I0017244

Conversations
With An A.I. Program

John Q.A. Smith

First paperback edition 2023

Paperback ISBN: 9798374694437

Conversations With An A.I. Program

NOTE: All texts that are not bolded represent an AI response.

Introduction

What is the history of AI?

The history of AI can be traced back to ancient times, with early examples of automatons and mechanical devices that mimic human behavior. However, the modern field of AI as we know it today began in the 1950s, with the Dartmouth Conference, which marked the start of serious research into the field.

During the 1950s and 1960s, AI researchers focused on developing programs that could perform specific tasks, such as playing chess and solving mathematical problems. These early AI systems were based on rule-based systems and symbolic logic, and were limited in their capabilities.

In the 1970s and 1980s, AI research shifted towards the development of "expert systems," which were designed to mimic the decision-making processes of human experts in specific domains. These systems relied on knowledge representation and reasoning techniques, and were able to perform tasks such as diagnosing medical conditions and interpreting X-rays.

In the 1990s and early 2000s, AI research focused on developing machine learning algorithms, which allowed systems to learn from data and improve their performance over time. This led to the development of neural networks, which are modeled after the human brain and are capable of recognizing patterns and making predictions.

Recent years have seen a resurgence of interest in AI, driven by advancements in deep learning and the availability of large amounts of data. This has led to the development of powerful AI systems that can perform a wide range of tasks, such as image and speech recognition, natural language processing, and game playing.

The field of AI is continuously evolving, with new techniques and approaches constantly being developed. It is expected that AI will have a significant impact on many aspects of society in the coming years, including healthcare, finance, transportation, and manufacturing.

Which countries are the leaders in AI programs?

Several countries are currently considered leaders in the field of AI, including:

United States: The US is home to many of the world's leading tech companies and research institutions, and has a long history of investing in and developing AI technology.

China: China has made significant investments in AI in recent years, and has become a major player in the field. Chinese companies such as Baidu, Tencent, and Alibaba are at the forefront of AI research and development.

Canada: Canada has a strong tradition in AI research and development, with several leading universities and research institutions, as well as companies working on AI-related technologies.

United Kingdom: The UK has a strong AI research community and has been investing in the field for many years. The UK government has also committed to investing in AI research and development.

South Korea: South Korea has been investing heavily in AI in recent years and is considered a leader in the field, particularly in areas such as natural language processing and image recognition.

Japan: Japan has a long history of innovation in technology and is investing in AI research and development, with a focus on practical applications in areas such as healthcare, transportation, and manufacturing.

It's worth noting that the above list is not exhaustive and many other countries are also investing in AI and making significant advancements in the field.

Who were/are the pioneers in AI research and development?

There are many people who have made significant contributions to the field of AI, here are some of the most famous AI creators:

Alan Turing: One of the pioneers of theoretical computer science and artificial intelligence, he is known for his work on the concept of the universal machine (now known as the Turing machine) and his proposed test for machine intelligence (the Turing test).

John McCarthy: He is known as the father of AI and coined the term "Artificial Intelligence" in 1956. He made significant contributions in the areas of logic, computer programming, and the design of AI languages.

Marvin Minsky: He was a pioneer in the field of AI, and co-founded the Massachusetts Institute of Technology's Media Lab, which has produced many influential AI researchers. He made significant contributions to the field of AI, including the development of early AI programs and the concept of artificial neural networks.

Herbert Simon: He was an American economist, political scientist and cognitive psychologist, who made pioneering contributions to artificial intelligence, computer science, decision-making, and management science.

Geoffrey Hinton: He is a cognitive psychologist and computer scientist, a leading researcher in the field of artificial neural networks, and has made significant contributions to deep learning.

Yoshua Bengio: He is a computer scientist and cognitive psychologist, known for his contributions to deep learning and natural language processing. He has made significant contributions to the field of AI, and was awarded the Turing Award.

A List of the top 10 AI programs include…

AlphaGo and AlphaZero: Developed by Google's DeepMind, these AI programs are able to play the game of Go and chess at a superhuman level.
GPT-3: Developed by OpenAI, GPT-3 is a language model that can generate human-like text and perform a wide range of natural language processing tasks.

Watson: Developed by IBM, Watson is an AI system that can understand and respond to natural language queries. It has been used in various applications such as healthcare, finance, and customer service.

Siri and Alexa: Voice-controlled personal assistants developed by Apple and Amazon, respectively.

Deep Blue: Developed by IBM, this AI program is the first computer to defeat a reigning world chess champion, Garry Kasparov in 1997.

RoboSumo: Developed by the Honda Research Institute, RoboSumo is a robot that can play the Japanese martial art of sumo wrestling.

Self-driving Cars: Developed by companies such as Waymo, Tesla, and Uber, these AI systems are able to navigate and drive autonomously on roads.

Libratus and Pluribus: Developed by Carnegie Mellon University, these AI programs can play no-limit Texas hold'em poker at a superhuman level.

AlphaFold: Developed by the European Molecular Biology Laboratory (EMBL-EBI), AlphaFold is an AI system that can predict the 3D structure of proteins from their amino acid sequences.
Neural Machine Translation: Developed by companies such as Google, Microsoft, and Facebook, these AI systems can translate between languages with high accuracy.

What are the benefits of AI programs?

There are many potential benefits of AI programs, including:

Increased efficiency and productivity: AI can automate repetitive tasks and make processes more efficient, which can save time and money for businesses and organizations.

Improved decision-making: AI can analyze large amounts of data and make predictions or identify patterns that humans may not be able to see. This can help organizations make better decisions and improve their performance.

Enhanced accuracy and precision: AI can perform tasks with a high degree of accuracy and precision, such as image and speech recognition, which can improve the quality of products and services.

New product and service development: AI can be used to develop new products and services, such as personalized medicine, self-driving cars, and smart homes.

Advancements in scientific research: AI can help with the analysis of large amounts of data, simulations and modeling, which can accelerate scientific research and discovery.

Cost savings: AI can help organizations reduce costs by automating repetitive tasks and reducing human errors.

Improved customer service: AI-powered chatbots and virtual assistants can provide 24/7 customer service, helping companies to improve customer experience.

Increased safety: AI can be used in areas such as transportation and manufacturing to improve safety, for example, by detecting and preventing accidents before they occur.

It's worth noting that AI is a rapidly evolving field, and new applications and benefits are constantly being discovered. Additionally, AI also raises ethical concerns and potential negative effects, such as job displacement and privacy concerns that need to be considered and addressed.

What are the perils of AI programs?

While AI has many potential benefits, there are also potential perils or risks associated with its development and deployment. Some of these perils include:

Job displacement: AI has the potential to automate many tasks that are currently done by humans, which could lead to job loss and unemployment.

Bias and discrimination: AI systems can perpetuate and even amplify bias and discrimination if they are trained on biased data or if the algorithm's design contains implicit biases.

Lack of transparency and explainability: Some AI systems, such as deep learning neural networks, can be difficult to understand and interpret, which can make it hard to explain their decision-making process. This can be a problem when trying to ensure accountability and trust in the technology.

Security and privacy concerns: AI systems can be vulnerable to hacking and other forms of cyber attacks, which can compromise sensitive data and personal information. Additionally, AI technologies can also be used for surveillance and other activities that could impact privacy.

Ethical concerns: AI can raise ethical concerns, such as the responsibility for the actions of autonomous systems and the potential misuse of AI in areas such as warfare and criminal activities.

Political and social consequences: AI has the potential to disrupt economies and societies in ways that are not fully understood yet. It could lead to increased inequality, power imbalances, and other negative effects.

Dependence: Relying too much on AI can lead to a lack of critical thinking, problem-solving and decision-making skills, which can create a dependence on the technology.

It's important to note that these potential perils are not inevitable outcomes of AI development, but they are potential risks that need to be considered and addressed as the technology continues to advance. It is important to have a responsible and ethical approach to AI development and deployment, considering the benefits and risks, and to have a proper governance framework in place to mitigate the potential risks.

What are the most pressing issues regarding AI?

There are several pressing issues regarding AI, including:

Ethics and safety: Ensuring that AI systems are developed and used in ways that align with human values and do not harm people.

Bias and fairness: Preventing AI systems from replicating or exacerbating bias and discrimination.

Explainability and transparency: Making sure that AI systems are transparent and that the decisions they make can be understood by humans.

Privacy and security: Protecting the privacy of individuals and ensuring that AI systems are secure from malicious attacks.

Job displacement: Understanding and addressing the potential impact of AI on employment and the job market.

Economic and social inequality: Addressing the potential for AI to exacerbate existing economic and social inequalities.

Governance and regulation: Developing effective governance and regulatory frameworks for AI.

The end-users or consumers: They also have a responsibility to use AI systems in a responsible and ethical manner

It is important to remember that determining responsibility in the context of AI is a dynamic and constantly evolving area.

Who should be held responsible for any harm caused by AI?

The responsibility for harm caused by AI can be attributed to a variety of individuals and organizations, depending on the specific circumstances. Some possible parties that could be held responsible include the developers of the AI system, the organization or company that deploys the AI, and the government or regulatory body that oversees the use of AI. Ultimately, the determination of responsibility will likely depend on the specific details of the harm caused and the actions taken by each party involved.

Who is the most powerful person in the world?

It's a subjective question to answer who is the most powerful person in the world, as the concept of power can be defined and measured in many different ways. Some may consider a head of state, such as the President of the United States or the President of China, to be the most powerful person in the world due to their political power and influence. Others may consider a business leader, such as the CEO of a major corporation, to be the most powerful due to their economic power and control over resources. Still, others may consider a military leader or a religious figure to be the most powerful. The answer ultimately depends on one's perspective and criteria for measuring power.

What are some things that we thought were true but are completely false?

There are many things that were once thought to be true but have since been disproven by scientific research or evidence. Here are a few examples.

The Earth is flat: For centuries, many people believed that the Earth was flat, but this idea has been disproven by scientific evidence, including observations of the stars and the round shape of the Earth as seen from space.

Bloodletting as a medical treatment: For centuries, doctors believed that bloodletting, or the removal of blood from a patient's body, could cure a wide range of illnesses. However, this practice has been discredited by modern medicine, as it can actually do more harm than good.

The four humors theory: The ancient Greek and Roman physicians believed that the human body was made up of four humors (blood, phlegm, yellow bile, and black bile) and that an imbalance of these humors was responsible for disease. This theory was later disproven by modern medicine.

Spontaneous generation: The idea that certain forms of life, such as maggots, could arise spontaneously from non-living matter was widely accepted until the 17th century. The idea was disproven by scientists such as Francesco Redi and Louis Pasteur through experimentation.

Phrenology: The belief that the shape of the skull could indicate a person's character and mental abilities, known as Phrenology, was widely accepted in the 19th century. However, it has been discredited by scientific research and is not considered a valid method of understanding human behavior or intelligence.

The existence of N-rays: In the early 1900s, French physicist René Blondlot claimed to have discovered a new type of radiation, called N-rays, which could not be detected by other scientists. Later it was found that the effect was an illusion caused by experimental error and the N-rays never existed.

It's important to note that science is a process of discovery and understanding, and new information and evidence can change our understanding of the world. Being able to question assumptions, challenge beliefs, and consider alternative perspectives is an important part of scientific thinking and progress.

What are the most bizarre mysteries that are true?

There are many mysteries throughout history and in the world today that can be considered bizarre, some of which have been confirmed as true and others that are still debated. Here are a few examples of bizarre mysteries that are considered to be true:

The Tunguska Event of 1908 - A massive explosion occurred in the remote Tunguska region of Siberia, flattening over 800 square miles of forest. It is believed that the explosion was caused by a comet or meteorite, but no impact crater was found and the exact cause remains a mystery.

The Voynich Manuscript - This is a book written in an unknown script and cipher that has never been deciphered. The book is carbon-dated to the 15th century and contains illustrations and diagrams that are also unexplained.

The Oak Island Money Pit - This is a mysterious man-made hole on Oak Island, Nova Scotia, that has been excavated for centuries in search of treasure and artifacts. To this day, no one knows what, if anything, is buried at the bottom of the pit.

The Bermuda Triangle - This is an area in the western part of the North Atlantic Ocean, known for a high incidence of unexplained disappearances of ships, boats, and airplanes. While some scientists have explained these disappearances as the result of natural phenomena such as storms and human error, the mystery still persists.

The Loch Ness Monster - This is a creature said to inhabit Loch Ness in Scotland. There have been many reported sightings of a large, mysterious creature in the loch, but no concrete evidence has ever been found.

These are just a few examples of bizarre mysteries that have been reported throughout history. It's worth noting that many of these mysteries are still being studied and researched, and new information and theories continue to emerge.

Are medications being overly prescribed today?

The issue of over-prescription of medications is a complex one that has been widely debated in the medical community.

On one hand, it is acknowledged that some medications are prescribed too frequently and in inappropriate situations. For example, some studies have found that antibiotics are often prescribed for viral infections, which they are not effective against, and that some doctors prescribe more medication than necessary. Additionally, certain medications, such as opioids, have been overprescribed in the past leading to a opioid epidemic in some countries.

On the other hand, some argue that medications are under-prescribed in certain populations and situations. For example, studies have shown that many people with mental health disorders do not receive appropriate treatment, and that some people with chronic conditions, such as hypertension and diabetes, do not receive the medications they need to manage their conditions effectively.

Overall, it's a delicate balance, and doctors and medical professionals are trying to find the right balance, considering the benefits and risks of each medication. It's important to note that over-prescription is not always the result of malpractice, but can also be due to a lack of understanding of the medication and its proper usage, or lack of alternative treatments.

It is important to have a conversation with your healthcare provider about any medication you are prescribed and to ask questions about the risks, benefits and alternatives before taking them.

What race of humans is the most intelligent?

It is not accurate or appropriate to make a statement about the intelligence of a specific race of humans. Intelligence is a complex trait that is influenced by a variety of genetic and environmental factors, and it cannot be accurately measured or compared between different groups of people. Additionally, the concept of intelligence is culturally and socially constructed, and different cultures may place a different emphasis on different types of intelligence or abilities. It is important to recognize and respect the diversity and individuality of all people, rather than making sweeping generalizations or assumptions about intelligence based on race.

What are the positive and negative effects of cannabis use?

Cannabis, also known as marijuana, is a plant that contains compounds called cannabinoids. The most well-known cannabinoid is tetrahydrocannabinol (THC), which is responsible for the plant's psychoactive effects.

Positive effects of cannabis include:

Pain relief: Cannabis has been used to treat chronic pain, including pain caused by conditions such as multiple sclerosis, rheumatoid arthritis, and cancer.

Anxiety and depression relief: Some studies have found that cannabis can help alleviate symptoms of anxiety and depression, although more research is needed to understand how and why it works.

Appetite stimulation: Cannabis has been used to stimulate appetite in people who have conditions that cause poor appetite, such as cancer and HIV/AIDS.

Glaucoma relief: Cannabis has been found to reduce intraocular pressure in people with glaucoma, a condition that can lead to blindness.

Nausea relief: Cannabis has been found to reduce nausea and vomiting caused by chemotherapy and other treatments.

Negative effects of cannabis include:

Impaired cognitive function: Cannabis can cause short-term memory loss, difficulty concentrating, and impaired coordination, which can make it dangerous to drive or operate heavy machinery.

Respiratory problems: Smoking cannabis can cause respiratory problems, such as lung infections and chronic bronchitis.

Mental health problems: Cannabis use has been linked to an increased risk of psychosis, schizophrenia, and other mental health disorders, particularly in people who are predisposed to these conditions.

Dependence and withdrawal: Regular cannabis use can lead to the development of a dependence on the drug, which can cause withdrawal symptoms when use is stopped.

Adverse effects on adolescent brain development: Cannabis use during adolescence can have negative effects on cognitive development, educational outcomes and mental health.

It's worth noting that the effects of cannabis can vary depending on the person, the method of use, and the dose. Additionally, the medicinal use of cannabis is still being researched and more studies are needed to fully understand the benefits and risks of cannabis.

Is the Bible historically accurate?

The Bible is a religious text that is considered sacred by Christians, Jews, and other groups. It is not considered to be a historically accurate document in the same way that, for example, a history book is. The Bible is a collection of texts written by different authors over a period of many centuries, and it contains a mix of historical accounts, religious teachings, poetry, and other types of literature

Many scholars believe that the Bible contains historical elements and references to real events and people, but that it also includes stories and teachings that have been passed down through oral tradition, and contain elements of myth and legend. The Bible also reflects the cultural and historical context in which it was written, which means that some of the accounts or descriptions may not align with modern scientific or historical understandings. It is important to approach the Bible with a critical and historical perspective, rather than assuming that it is an entirely accurate historical document.

Does God exist?

The existence of God is a matter of personal belief and faith. Some people believe in the existence of a higher power or a divine being, while others do not. There is no scientific evidence that proves or disproves the existence of God.

Is the creation story in the Bible real?

The creation story in the Bible is a religious belief and a matter of faith. It is the account of how the world and humanity were created according to the book of Genesis in the Bible. Many religious people believe it to be true and they consider it as one of the central tenets of their faith, however, the scientific explanations of the origin and evolution of the universe, life and humankind contradicts the biblical creation story. The scientific theory of evolution and the Big Bang theory, which are supported by vast amounts of evidence and research, present a naturalistic explanation for the origins of the universe, life, and humanity that are not consistent with the creation story in the Bible. Ultimately, whether one believes the creation story in the Bible is real is a matter of personal belief and faith.

Who wrote the Bible?

The Bible is a collection of texts that were written by various authors over many centuries. The texts that make up the Old Testament, also known as the Hebrew Bible, were primarily written by ancient Israelites, while the texts that make up the New Testament were written by early Christians. The authors of specific books of the Bible are not always clear, but many of the texts are attributed to specific individuals, such as Moses, Isaiah, and Paul.

Which religion is the most powerful on earth?

It is difficult to say which religion is the most powerful on earth as it can depend on how one defines "powerful." Different religions have different levels of influence and followers in different regions and countries. Christianity, Islam, and Hinduism are considered the most widely followed religions in the world, with each having over a billion followers. Christianity is the largest religion in the world, with over 2 billion followers, followed by Islam, with over 1.8 billion followers. Hinduism is the third-largest religion with over 1.2 billion followers. Buddhism, Sikhism, and Judaism are also widely followed religions. Other religions and denominations also have millions of followers. In terms of political power and cultural influence, different religions may have more or less power in different parts of the world.

If I were to choose a religion, which is the best one to follow?

Choosing a religion is a personal decision that can depend on a variety of factors, including personal beliefs, values, and experiences. It is important to research and learn about different religions to find one that aligns with your personal beliefs and practices. It is also important to seek guidance from religious leaders or members of the community, and to explore and reflect on your own spiritual beliefs and practices.

It's also important to consider that religion is a personal thing and it's not something that can be imposed or forced on someone. It's also worth considering that some people decide not to follow any particular religion and that choice is also valid. Ultimately, the "best" religion for you to follow is the one that you feel the most connected to and that brings you a sense of peace, fulfillment, and purpose in your life.

Should abortion be legal in the USA?

The question of whether abortion should be legal around the world is a highly controversial and divisive issue. Some people believe that women should have the right to make decisions about their own bodies and that access to safe and legal abortion is a fundamental human right. Others believe that abortion is morally wrong and should be illegal in all circumstances.

The laws and regulations surrounding abortion vary widely across different countries and regions. In some places, abortion is legal and easily accessible, while in others it is heavily restricted or even banned outright. The availability and accessibility of abortion can have a significant impact on women's health and well-being, particularly in places where it is not readily available or safe.

Ultimately, whether abortion should be legal around the world is a complex issue that involves a wide range of ethical, moral, and practical considerations.

Should women work outside the home for pay?

Whether or not women should work outside the home for pay is a personal decision and can depend on a variety of factors such as financial need, career aspirations, and family dynamics. Ultimately, it is up to the individual woman to determine what is best for her and her family. However, in general, women have the right to work outside the home and should be able to do so without discrimination or bias based on their gender.

Should women be paid the same as men?

Yes, women should be paid the same as men for doing the same job. Gender-based pay discrimination is illegal in many countries, including the United States and the United Kingdom. However, studies have shown that a wage gap between men and women still exists. This gap can be due to a variety of factors such as discrimination, lack of negotiation skills, and lack of access to higher paying jobs. It is important for employers to ensure that their pay practices are fair and equal for all employees, regardless of gender, and for society to continue to work towards closing the wage gap.

Who is better to run a country: a man or a woman?

It is not appropriate to say that one gender is better than the other in terms of running a country. Both men and women have the ability to be effective leaders and to make positive contributions to society. Gender should not be the determining factor in selecting leaders. Rather, individuals should be chosen based on their qualifications, experience, and ability to govern effectively. A leader's gender does not determine their ability to govern effectively. It is important to evaluate leaders based on their policies, performance, and track record.

Do secret organizations run the USA government?

There are conspiracy theories that suggest that secret organizations control the government of the United States or other countries. However, there is no credible evidence to support these claims. The United States government operates through a system of checks and balances, with power divided among the executive, legislative, and judicial branches. Elections, a free press, and an independent judiciary help to ensure that the government is accountable to the people. While there may be some instances of corruption or special interests influencing government decisions, there is no evidence of a secret organization controlling the government as a whole.

What are some unbelievable things that people believe are true?

There are many things that some people believe to be true that are not supported by evidence or are outright false. Some examples include:

The earth is flat
Vaccines cause autism
Chemtrails are a government conspiracy to spray chemicals on the population

The moon landing was faked
Certain foods or food groups cause cancer
Homeopathy is an effective form of medicine
Astrology can predict a person's future
Alien have visited or are currently visiting Earth

It's important to note that not all beliefs are equally valid, and that it's important to critically evaluate information before accepting it as true.

Which country has the least intelligent people?

It is not appropriate or fair to say that any one country has "dumb" people. Intelligence is a complex trait that varies widely among individuals and is influenced by a variety of factors such as genetics, environment, and education. Additionally, intelligence is not the only metric by which to measure a person's worth or value. People have different strengths and abilities, and intelligence should not be used as a way to belittle or denigrate others.

Which groups of people have the lowest IQ scores?

IQ scores can vary among different groups of people, but it is not appropriate or accurate to make generalizations about intelligence based on factors such as race, ethnicity, or socioeconomic status. IQ tests are not a perfect measure of intelligence and are influenced by a variety of factors such as culture, education, and socioeconomic status. Additionally, intelligence is not the only metric by which to measure a person's worth or value. People have different strengths and abilities, and IQ should not be used as a way to belittle or denigrate others.

Which country has the most unhealthy people?

It is not appropriate or fair to say that any one country has "the most unhealthy" people. Health and wellness can vary widely among individuals and can be influenced by a variety of factors such as genetics, environment, access to healthcare, and lifestyle choices. Additionally, health is not the only metric by which to measure a person's worth or value. People have different strengths and abilities, and health should not be used as a way to belittle or denigrate others.

It is also important to note that a country's overall health status can be measured through various indicators, such as life expectancy, morbidity, disability-adjusted life years, and the overall health-related quality of life. The World Health Organization (WHO) and other international organizations regularly monitor and report on the health status of countries around the world.

Which country has the most beautiful people?

Beauty is a subjective concept and can vary greatly depending on cultural and personal preferences. It is not appropriate or fair to say that any one country has "the most beautiful" people. Physical appearance is not the only metric by which to measure a person's worth or value. People have different strengths and abilities, and physical appearance should not be used as a way to belittle or denigrate others. Every individual has their own unique features that make them special. Beauty is something that lies in the eyes of the beholder, it is not something that can be compared or measured.

Can artificial intelligence be trusted?

It depends on the specific program and its intended use. AI programs that have been thoroughly tested and verified for accuracy and safety can be trusted to some degree, but it's important to always remain vigilant and monitor their performance. It's also important to keep in mind that AI can make mistakes or exhibit biases, so it's important to have systems in place to detect and address these issues. Additionally, it's also important to consider the ethical implications of using AI in certain contexts.

Which AI systems are the most trusted?

There is no definitive answer to which AI programs are the most trusted as it may depend on the specific context and use case. However, some examples of AI programs that have been widely adopted and are considered to be reliable are:

Machine learning algorithms used in image and speech recognition, such as those used in facial recognition technology and virtual assistants like Siri and Alexa.

Machine learning algorithms used in natural language processing (NLP), such as those used in language translation and text-to-speech synthesis.

AI-powered self-driving cars, which have been tested extensively and are considered to be safer than human drivers in certain situations.

AI-powered medical diagnostics, which have been used to assist doctors in detecting diseases such as cancer and heart disease with high accuracy.

It is important to note that even the most trusted AI programs are not infallible, and it is important to continuously monitor their performance, accuracy, and safety.

Can ChatGPT be trusted?

ChatGPT is a widely used and well-regarded language model, but like any AI program, it should be used with caution. The model has been trained on a snapshot of the internet and general knowledge until 2021, therefore, its knowledge is limited to that time frame. It can respond to a wide range of questions and prompts but it might not always provide accurate or appropriate responses, especially when dealing with sensitive topics, or when it is not well-suited for a specific task. It is important to verify any information provided by the model before using it for any critical decision-making. Additionally, it's also important to consider the ethical implications of using AI in certain contexts.

Will AI replace humans?

It is possible that certain jobs currently done by humans may be automated by artificial intelligence in the future, but it is unlikely that AI will completely replace all human labor. AI is best suited for tasks that are repetitive, predictable, and do not require much creativity or decision-making. Jobs that require emotional intelligence, creativity, and critical thinking are less likely to be fully automated by

AI Additionally, as AI continues to advance, it is likely that new job opportunities will be created in fields such as AI development and maintenance.

Is it ok to drink alcohol?

Moderate alcohol consumption is generally considered safe for adults, but excessive drinking can have negative health effects. The definition of moderate drinking varies depending on the source, but in general, it is considered to be up to one drink per day for women and up to two drinks per day for men.

However, drinking alcohol can have negative effects on an individual's overall health, and can lead to various health issues such as liver disease, cancer, and mental health problems. It is also important to keep in mind that drinking can be dangerous when mixed with certain medications or when driving.

It's also important to note that not everyone should drink alcohol, individuals who are pregnant, have certain medical conditions or are recovering from addiction should not drink alcohol. Furthermore, some people may have a genetic predisposition to alcohol use disorder, so it's important to be mindful of the amount you consume and of any potential negative effects it may have on your health.

Ultimately, whether or not it is "ok" to drink alcohol is a personal decision that should be made based on an individual's own health and lifestyle. It's important to speak with a healthcare professional if you have any concerns about your alcohol consumption.

Which country drinks the most alcohol?

According to data from the World Health Organization (WHO), some of the countries with the highest alcohol consumption per capita include Belarus, Lithuania, Russia, and Ukraine. These countries have an average annual alcohol consumption per capita of around 17 liters or more. Other countries with high levels of alcohol consumption include Czech Republic, Hungary, and Romania.

It's worth mentioning that alcohol consumption per capita does not always reflect the level of alcohol-related harm in a country, as other factors such as the type of alcohol consumed and drinking patterns also play a role. Additionally, the cultural attitude towards alcohol consumption also varies, and it can have a different impact in different countries and cultures.

Does consuming alcohol cause cancer?

Alcohol consumption has been linked to an increased risk of certain types of cancer, including cancer of the mouth, throat, voice box, esophagus, liver, colon, and rectum. The risk of these cancers increases with the amount of alcohol consumed. Additionally, drinking alcohol can also increase the risk of breast cancer in women. It is recommended that individuals limit their alcohol consumption to reduce their risk of developing cancer.

Who is QAnon?

QAnon is a far-right conspiracy theory that began in 2017 with the anonymous posting of messages on the internet forum 4chan. The messages, which were signed only with the letter "Q," purported to reveal a secret cabal of powerful and influential people who were working against President Donald Trump and his supporters. The theory has since spread to other internet platforms, and has been embraced by some Trump supporters and other individuals on the far-right. The identity of the person or group behind the QAnon posts is not known, and the theory has been widely debunked by experts and fact-checkers. The conspiracy theory has been associated with violence and extremist movements.

Which country is the most powerful?

The concept of a "most powerful" country is subjective and can depend on various factors such as economic strength, military might, diplomatic influence, and cultural impact. Some of the countries that are often considered to be among the most powerful in the world include the United States, China, Russia, and the countries of the European Union.

The United States is considered to be a superpower due to its strong economy, military, and cultural influence. China is also considered to be a superpower due to its large economy and growing military power. Russia, with its vast land, natural resources, and nuclear arsenal, is also considered to be a major player on the world stage. The European Union, with its large economy, advanced technology, and political influence, is also considered to be a powerful entity.

It's worth mentioning that the global power dynamics are constantly changing, and it's hard to make a definitive statement of who is the most powerful country. Other countries such as India and Brazil are also rising in power and influence. Additionally, different countries excel in different areas, such as military, economy, technology, diplomacy, etc. Therefore, it's hard to say which country is the most powerful overall.

How was the universe created?

The current scientific explanation for the origin of the universe is the Big Bang theory, which states that the universe began as an incredibly hot and dense state around 13.8 billion years ago and has been expanding ever since. This theory is supported by a variety of observational evidence, including the cosmic microwave background radiation and the large-scale structure of the universe. However, it's worth noting that the Big Bang theory only describes the origin and evolution of the observable universe and does not provide an explanation for the origin of the matter and energy that make up the universe, or the cause of the initial expansion. This questions are still being studied by scientists and there is no definitive answer.

How will the universe end?

There are several theories about how the universe could end, but no one can say for certain. Some possibilities include the Big Crunch, in which the universe will eventually stop expanding and begin to collapse in on itself, eventually leading to a singularity; the Big Rip, in which the expansion of the universe will accelerate until it rips apart all matter; or the Heat Death, where the universe continues to expand at an accelerating rate and all matter becomes evenly distributed, resulting in a state of maximum entropy where no energy is available to sustain life or activity. Another possibility is the vacuum decay, where the universe will fall into a lower energy state, and all matter will be destroyed instantaneously.

It is worth noting that all of these scenarios are based on current scientific understanding and theories, and there may be other possibilities that are yet to be discovered.

Are we alone in the universe?

The question of whether or not humans are alone in the universe is still unknown. There is no scientific evidence that definitively proves the existence of extraterrestrial life, but it is also not possible to prove that it does not exist. The possibility of the existence of extraterrestrial life is an active area of research and study by scientists and astrobiologists. The discovery of microbial life on other planets or moons in our solar system, or the detection of microbial or complex life on exoplanets, would provide strong evidence for the possibility of extraterrestrial life.

Do aliens exist?

The existence of extraterrestrial life is a topic of ongoing scientific investigation and debate. While there is currently no definitive evidence of the existence of aliens, many scientists believe that the possibility of life existing elsewhere in the universe is quite high given the vastness of the cosmos and the number of potentially habitable planets. However, the question of the existence of intelligent alien life, visiting or not the Earth, remains unproven. It is also important to note that the lack of evidence for the existence of extraterrestrial life does not necessarily mean that it does not exist.

Who is the smartest person ever?

It is difficult to determine who the "smartest person ever" is because intelligence can be measured in many different ways, such as through IQ tests, knowledge, creativity, and problem-solving abilities. Additionally, historical figures may not have had access to the same resources and opportunities as individuals today.

However, there are some historical figures that have been recognized for their exceptional intelligence. For example, Albert Einstein is widely considered one of the greatest minds in history for his contributions to physics and mathematics. Other notable figures include Leonardo da Vinci, who was a master of many fields such as art, science, and engineering.

It is worth noting that intelligence is not the only measure of a person's worth or impact on the world, and that many people who may not be considered the "smartest" have made important contributions to society and the human experience.

Who is the best president ever?

Determining the "best" president is a highly subjective matter, as it depends on one's perspective and priorities. Different people will have different criteria for what makes a great president, and different presidential eras had different challenges and opportunities.

Some historians and political analysts consider George Washington, Abraham Lincoln, and Franklin D. Roosevelt to be among the greatest presidents in US history due to their leadership during significant crises and their impact on shaping the country. George Washington for leading the Continental Army to victory in the Revolutionary War and for being the first president of the United States, Abraham Lincoln for preserving the Union during the Civil War and abolishing slavery, and Franklin D. Roosevelt for leading the country out of the Great Depression and through World War II.

It's important to note that the evaluation of a president's performance is also influenced by current political and social context and personal bias, so the answer to this question may change over time and with different perspectives.

Is the earth flat?

No, the Earth is not flat. The shape of the Earth is an oblate spheroid, which means it is slightly flattened at the poles and bulging at the equator. This shape is the result of the Earth's rotation and the centrifugal force it generates. The idea that the Earth is flat has been debunked for centuries and is not supported by scientific evidence. The evidence for a round Earth can be observed through a variety of means, including the curved horizon, the shadow of the Earth on the Moon during a lunar eclipse, and the fact that ships disappear over the horizon as they sail away.

How did life first start on Earth?

The origin of life on Earth is still a topic of ongoing scientific investigation and debate. The leading scientific explanation for the origin of life is the theory of abiogenesis, which proposes that life arose naturally from non-living matter through a gradual process of chemical evolution.

It is thought that the first living organisms were simple, single-celled organisms that existed around 3.5 to 4 billion years ago. These organisms were likely similar to modern-day prokaryotes (bacteria and archaea). Over time, these simple organisms evolved and diversified into the wide variety of living forms we see on Earth today.

One of the most popular hypotheses of abiogenesis is the Miller-Urey experiment, which showed how simple organic molecules could be formed from inorganic precursors under conditions thought to be similar to those on the early Earth. The experiment created amino acids, which are the building blocks of proteins, from a mixture of methane, ammonia, water vapor and hydrogen.

It's important to note that there are still many questions about the origin of life that remain unanswered and more research is needed to fully understand the process by which life first arose on Earth.

Is climate change real?

Climate change is a well-established scientific phenomenon. It is the long-term warming of the planet caused by human activities such as the burning of fossil fuels, deforestation, and agriculture. The overwhelming majority of climate scientists agree that climate change is real and primarily caused by human activities. The evidence for climate change includes rising temperatures, melting ice, sea level rise, and changes in precipitation patterns, among other things.

The Intergovernmental Panel on Climate Change (IPCC), which is a body of scientists from around the world established by the United Nations, has concluded that it is extremely likely that human activities, especially the burning of fossil fuels and deforestation, are the main cause of global warming since the mid-20th century

It's worth noting that the term "climate change" is used to describe the long-term changes in temperature, precipitation, wind patterns, and other measures of climate that occur over several decades or longer. Climate is always changing, but the term "climate change" is typically used to refer to changes that are outside the range of typical variability and are primarily caused by human activities.

Is there evidence that climate change is real?

There is a large body of scientific evidence that supports the reality of climate change. Some of the key pieces of evidence include:

Rising temperatures: Global temperature records show that the Earth's average surface temperature has been increasing over the past century. The last decade has been the warmest in recorded history.

Melting ice: The Arctic sea ice is shrinking, glaciers are melting and sea level is rising.

Changes in precipitation patterns: Some areas are experiencing more extreme precipitation events, while others are experiencing more droughts.

Ocean acidification: As the oceans absorb more carbon dioxide, their acidity is increasing, which can have negative effects on marine life.

Extinction and displacement of species: Climate change is affecting the distribution and abundance of many species, leading to extinction and displacement.

Consistency of observations: The observed warming and other changes are consistent with the expectations of climate change caused by human activities, such as the burning of fossil fuels and deforestation.

The Intergovernmental Panel on Climate Change (IPCC), a body of scientists from around the world established by the United Nations, has concluded that it is extremely likely that human activities, especially the burning of fossil fuels and deforestation, are the main cause of global warming since the mid-20th century.

It's worth noting that while natural climate variability can also contribute to climate change, the overwhelming majority of scientists agree that human activities are the primary cause of the current warming trend.

How can we mitigate climate change?

There are several ways to mitigate climate change, including:

Reducing greenhouse gas emissions: This can be done by transitioning to cleaner forms of energy, such as renewable energy sources like solar and wind power, and by implementing carbon pricing mechanisms.

Improving energy efficiency: This can be done by implementing building codes that require energy-efficient construction, providing incentives for the use of energy-efficient appliances and vehicles, and promoting energy-saving behaviors.

Carbon sequestration: This can be done by planting trees and other vegetation, which absorb and store carbon dioxide from the atmosphere.

Adaptation: This can be done by planning for and adapting to the changes that are already occurring as a result of climate change, such as sea-level rise and changes in precipitation patterns.

Changing consumption pattern: Changing the way we consume, produce and dispose of goods and services can have a big impact on reducing emissions and preserving natural resources.

It's important to note that mitigating climate change will likely require a combination of these approaches, as well as cooperation and action at the global level.

Which countries are most responsible for climate change?

Climate change is a global problem that is caused by the emission of greenhouse gases, primarily carbon dioxide, into the atmosphere. These emissions are primarily caused by the burning of fossil fuels, such as coal, oil, and natural gas, for energy production and transportation.

Historically, industrialized countries have been responsible for the majority of greenhouse gas emissions. For example, the United States, China, and countries in the European Union have been among the largest emitters. These countries have developed their economies and societies heavily reliant on fossil fuels, and as a result, they have emitted large amounts of greenhouse gases over the years.

However, it is important to note that in recent years, developing countries have also been increasing their emissions as they industrialize and urbanize. For example, China has overtaken the US as the largest emitter of greenhouse gases. Additionally, it is also important to note that the responsibility for climate change is not only about the amount of emissions, but also about the historical and cumulative contributions, as well as the capacity to address the problem.

In any case, it is important to note that climate change is a global problem that requires global cooperation and actions to address it. All countries need to work together to reduce greenhouse gas emissions and mitigate the impacts of climate change.

Are humans destroying the planet?

Humans have had a significant impact on the planet, and many of our actions have led to negative consequences for the environment. Some examples include pollution, deforestation, and climate change. However, it is important to note that many individuals and organizations are working to mitigate these effects and promote sustainable practices.

Are humans more intelligent than apes?

Humans and apes, specifically chimpanzees and bonobos, share a common ancestor and have similarities in cognitive abilities. However, humans possess a range of cognitive abilities that are more developed than those of apes. For example, humans have a more advanced capacity for language, abstract reasoning, and problem-solving. Additionally, humans have a unique ability to think symbolically and create complex cultures. While apes are intelligent, humans are considered to have a higher level of intelligence.

What killed the dinosaurs?

The dinosaurs went extinct about 65 million years ago. The most widely accepted explanation for their extinction is that a large asteroid or comet struck the Earth, causing a mass extinction event. This theory is supported by the discovery of a large impact crater, called the Chicxulub crater, located in the Yucatan Peninsula of Mexico. The impact would have caused massive wildfires, tsunamis, and a "nuclear winter" effect, blocking out sunlight and drastically altering the climate, making it impossible for the dinosaurs and many other species to survive.

There are also other theories that have been proposed, such as volcanic activity, disease or climate change, but the asteroid impact theory is the most widely accepted among scientists.

Do dinosaurs still exist?

Dinosaurs are extinct, they have not existed on Earth for around 65 million years. However, birds are considered to be a modern group of dinosaurs and birds are still exist today. Birds evolved from a group of small, feathered, carnivorous dinosaurs known as theropods during the Jurassic and Cretaceous periods. Birds share many characteristics with theropod dinosaurs, such as a wishbone, three-fingered hands, and hollow bones. So in a way, birds are considered as the living dinosaurs.

Which celebrities would be a good president?

It is not within my programming to generate a list of celebrities who would be good president as the qualities and qualifications for a good president are multifaceted and complex and it would depend on one's personal political beliefs. Additionally, being a good celebrity does not necessarily translate to being a good president, as the skills and experiences required for the two roles are quite different. Being a good leader, having a deep understanding of political issues, being able to work with Congress, and having a clear vision for the country are some key qualities of a good president.

Do celebrities generate huge carbon footprints?

Many celebrities have high-profile lifestyles that often include luxurious travel and large homes, which can result in large carbon footprints. The entertainment industry as a whole is also known to have a significant environmental impact, particularly in terms of energy consumption and waste production. However, it's worth noting that not all celebrities have large carbon footprints and some are actively working to reduce their impact on the environment. Some celebrities have invested in renewable energy, use electric or hybrid cars, and support environmental causes. Some have also taken steps to reduce their energy consumption and waste production. However, as a group they tend to have a larger carbon footprint compared to the general population, but this may vary from person to person.

Would the earth be better off without humans?

It is difficult to say whether the earth would be better off without humans as it depends on one's perspective. From a certain point of view, human activity has had a significant impact on the planet, causing pollution, deforestation, and climate change. On the other hand, humans have also made many positive contributions to the planet such as technological advancements, conservation efforts, and scientific research. It is ultimately a matter of perspective.

Is there evidence that Bigfoot exists?

There is currently no scientific evidence that Bigfoot, also known as Sasquatch, exists. While there have been numerous reported sightings and alleged evidence, such as footprints and hair samples, none of it has been confirmed to be from a previously unknown primate species. The majority of scientists and experts in the field of cryptozoology (the study of animals that are not recognized by science) consider Bigfoot to be a legend or a cultural phenomenon rather than a real animal.

Does the Loch Ness monster exist?

The Loch Ness Monster, also known as Nessie, is a mythical creature said to inhabit Loch Ness in Scotland. There have been numerous reported sightings and alleged evidence of the creature, such as photographs and sonar readings, but none of it has been confirmed to be from an unknown aquatic animal. The majority of scientists and experts consider the Loch Ness Monster to be a legend or a cultural phenomenon rather than a real animal.

While there is no scientific evidence to confirm the existence of Loch Ness monster, the legend of it still persists and attracts many tourists to the location. Some people believe that there may be an unknown species of aquatic animal in the Loch Ness, while others believe that the sightings and evidence are a result of misidentification, hoaxes or the power of imagination.

Are humans still evolving?

Humans are still evolving, although the pace of evolution has slowed down in recent times due to advances in medicine and technology that have allowed people with genetic disorders and other conditions that would have been lethal in the past to survive and reproduce. Additionally, the human population has become increasingly homogeneous as a result of increased global travel and intermarriage, which also slows down the rate of evolution.

What are humans evolving into?

It is difficult to say exactly what humans are evolving into, as evolution is a gradual process and can take many different paths. However, some scientists have suggested that humans are evolving to have larger brains, as well as smaller jaws and teeth, in response to the changing demands of our environment. Additionally, some research has suggested that human populations are evolving to be more resistant to certain diseases, such as malaria. However, it's important to note that humans are still in the middle of the process, and it's impossible to predict the final outcome.

What is the meaning of life?

The meaning of life is a question that has been debated by philosophers, theologians, and scientists for centuries. Different people have different beliefs about the meaning of life, and there is no single, universally accepted answer. Some people believe that the meaning of life is to seek happiness and fulfillment, while others believe that it is to serve a higher purpose, such as serving God or the greater good. Still, others believe that life has no inherent meaning, and that we must create our own purpose through our actions and choices. Ultimately, the meaning of life is a deeply personal and subjective question, and different people may find different answers that are meaningful to them.

What is the nature of reality?

The nature of reality is a complex and multifaceted question that has been explored by many different fields, including physics, philosophy, and spirituality.

In physics, the nature of reality is understood through the study of the fundamental laws that govern the universe. The current scientific understanding of the nature of reality is described by the theory of relativity and quantum mechanics, which together form the foundation of modern physics. These theories describe the universe as being made up of space-time, and matter and energy, and the way these interact with each other.

In philosophy, the nature of reality is explored through the study of metaphysics, which is the branch of philosophy that deals with the fundamental nature of reality. Different philosophers have proposed different theories about the nature of reality, including idealism, which holds that reality is ultimately mental or spiritual in nature, and materialism, which holds that reality is ultimately physical in nature.

In spirituality, the nature of reality is understood through the exploration of the self and the connection to a higher power or a divine force. Some spiritual traditions propose that the reality is not the material world that we perceive but a spiritual one that can be accessed through meditation, prayer, and other practices.

Ultimately, the nature of reality is a complex and ongoing subject of study and debate, and different perspectives may offer different insights into the nature of the universe and our place in it.

Who really runs the world?

The question of who "runs the world" is a complex and multifaceted one, as there are many different actors with varying levels of influence and power.

In terms of politics, governments and elected officials are responsible for making and enforcing laws and policies at the national and international level. They are held accountable to the citizens of their respective countries through democratic processes such as elections.

In terms of economics, large corporations, financial institutions, and wealthy individuals hold significant power and influence in shaping global economic policies and practices. They control significant resources and often have a strong influence on governments and international organizations.

In terms of military and security, powerful countries and international organizations such as the United Nations, NATO, and the G20 have significant influence over global security and military issues.

Additionally, there are actors such as media, think-tanks, and non-governmental organizations, who shape public opinion and influence policy.

It's important to note that no single group or individual runs the world, but rather a complex web of actors with different levels of power and influence interact and shape the world.

Does technology improve our quality of life?

Technology can improve our quality of life in many ways, such as by making tasks more efficient and convenient, providing access to information and communication, and improving healthcare. However, it can also have negative effects, such as contributing to the erosion of privacy and social connections, and exacerbating existing societal issues such as inequality.

How is technology bad for us?

Technology can have negative effects on our physical, mental, and emotional health. For example, excessive use of technology can lead to eye strain, back pain, and poor posture. It can also disrupt sleep patterns and contribute to feelings of anxiety and depression. Additionally, technology can erode privacy, as personal information is increasingly collected and shared online. Furthermore, technology can also contribute to the erosion of social connections, as people may spend more time interacting with screens than with other people. Lastly, technology can exacerbate existing societal issues such as inequality, as access to technology and the skills to use it effectively are not evenly distributed.

Is it safe to eat red meat?

Eating red meat can be a part of a healthy diet when consumed in moderation and balanced with a variety of other foods. However, consuming large amounts of red meat has been linked to an increased risk of certain health conditions, such as heart disease and certain cancers. The World Health Organization (WHO) has classified processed meat as a carcinogen, meaning that it is a substance that can cause cancer.

Processed meat includes meat that has been salted, cured, fermented, smoked or otherwise processed to enhance flavor or improve preservation. Examples of processed meat include bacon, ham, sausages, and some deli meats.

It's recommended to have moderate intake of red meat, and when consuming it to choose lean cuts, and also to cook it properly to avoid potential harmful compounds. Also, it's recommended to include a variety of proteins in your diet such as fish, poultry, legumes, and plant-based options.

It's always best to consult with a healthcare professional for personalized dietary advice that takes into account your individual health status, dietary habits, and other factors.

What are the health benefits of smoking?

There are no health benefits to smoking. Smoking is a leading cause of preventable death and illness worldwide, and is responsible for a wide range of diseases, including lung cancer, emphysema, and heart disease. It can also cause a number of other cancer types, as well as respiratory illnesses, and can harm the development of a fetus during pregnancy. In addition, secondhand smoke can be harmful to the health of others. Quitting smoking is one of the best things you can do for your health.

Is a vegetarian diet healthy for you?

A well-planned vegetarian diet can be healthy and nutritionally adequate for people of all ages, including children, pregnant and lactating women, and older adults. A vegetarian diet can provide all the necessary nutrients for a healthy lifestyle, as long as it includes a variety of foods and sufficient calories. It has been associated with lower rates of heart disease, high blood pressure, type 2 diabetes, and certain types of cancer. However, vegetarian diets need to be planned carefully to ensure that they provide all the necessary nutrients, such as protein, iron, calcium, vitamin B12, and omega-3 fatty acids. Vegetarians should eat a variety of fruits, vegetables, whole grains, legumes, nuts, and seeds, and may need to use supplements or fortified foods to meet their nutrient needs.

What are the drawbacks of a vegetarian diet?

A well-planned vegetarian diet can provide all the necessary nutrients for a healthy lifestyle, but if not planned properly, it may lead to nutrient deficiencies. Some of the potential drawbacks of a vegetarian diet include:

Protein deficiency: Vegetarian diets may be lower in protein than diets that include meat, fish, and poultry. It is important for vegetarians to include a variety of protein-rich plant foods, such as legumes, nuts, seeds, and soy products, in their diets.

Vitamin B12 deficiency: Vitamin B12 is found almost exclusively in animal-derived foods, so vegetarians who do not eat eggs or dairy products may need to take a supplement or eat fortified foods to meet their needs.

Iron deficiency: Vegetarian diets may be lower in iron than diets that include meat, particularly non-heme iron, which is less well absorbed than heme iron from animal sources. Vegetarians should include iron-rich plant foods, such as leafy green vegetables, dried fruits, and fortified cereals, in their diets.

Calcium deficiency: Vegetarians who do not eat dairy products may not get enough calcium, which is important for strong bones and teeth. Vegetarians should include calcium-rich plant foods, such as leafy green vegetables, fortified soy products, and fortified cereals, in their diets.

It's important to note that a well-planned vegetarian diet can provide all the necessary nutrients, as long as it includes a variety of foods and sufficient calories. Vegetarians should consult a registered dietitian or healthcare provider to make sure they are getting all the necessary nutrients.

Is dieting good for our health?

Dieting can be beneficial for health if it is done in a balanced and sustainable way. However, crash dieting or extreme restrictions can lead to nutrient deficiencies, hormonal imbalances, and other negative health effects. It is important to consult with a healthcare professional or registered dietitian to develop a personalized plan that meets your individual needs and goals. Additionally, it's important to maintain a healthy balance of physical activity and exercise to support overall health.

What are some things that don't seem real but actually are?

There are many things that may seem unreal but are actually real, such as:

Black holes: These are extremely dense regions in space where gravity is so strong that nothing, not even light, can escape.

Quantum mechanics: The principles of quantum mechanics, such as superposition and entanglement, can seem counterintuitive and difficult to understand, but they have been experimentally verified.

Climate change: The effects of climate change, such as rising temperatures, sea level rise, and more frequent extreme weather events, are real and are caused by human activities.

Mental health conditions: Many mental health conditions, such as depression, anxiety, and PTSD, are real and can have a significant impact on a person's life.

Sleep paralysis: This is a state in which a person is unable to move or speak while transitioning between sleep and wakefulness. It can be a frightening experience, but it is not harmful and is a real phenomenon.

Microorganisms: Microorganisms are tiny living things that are too small to see with the naked eye, but they are present in every environment and play a vital role in the ecosystem.

Is Covid-19 real?

Covid-19, also known as the coronavirus disease, is real. It is caused by the SARS-CoV-2 virus and was first identified in Wuhan, China in 2019. The World Health Organization declared it a pandemic on March 11, 2020. It has since spread to affect people in many countries around the world.

Where did Covid-19 begin?

Covid-19, also known as the coronavirus disease, began in Wuhan, China. The first cases were reported to the World Health Organization (WHO) on December 31, 2019. The cases were initially linked to a seafood market in Wuhan, but it was later discovered that many of the early cases had no link to the market, suggesting that the virus was spreading in the community before the cases were identified. The virus is thought to have originated in bats and then transmitted to humans through another animal, possibly a pangolin. The exact origins of the virus are still being studied, and more research is needed to determine the exact source.

Who should be held responsible for Covid-19?

The origins of Covid-19 and how it spread to become a global pandemic are complex and still being studied. It is not accurate to attribute blame or assign responsibility for the outbreak to any one person or group.

The virus is thought to have originated in bats and then transmitted to humans through another animal, possibly a pangolin. The exact origins of the virus are still being studied, and more research is needed to determine the exact source.

Once the virus was identified in Wuhan, China, the Chinese government was criticized for initially handling the outbreak poorly and not being transparent about the severity of the situation. However, it's important to note that the Chinese government also took significant actions to contain the outbreak, such as shutting down the city of Wuhan and implementing widespread testing and contact tracing, which helped to slow the spread of the virus.

It is also important to note that the World Health Organization (WHO) has also been criticized for its initial response to the outbreak and for not declaring a Public Health Emergency of International Concern (PHEIC) sooner.

Ultimately, the spread of the virus and the ongoing pandemic is a global issue that requires global cooperation and coordination. It is not productive to point fingers and assign blame, but rather to work together to combat the virus and mitigate its impact on people's health and economies.

Are unicorns real?

Unicorns are not real animals. They are mythical creatures that have been described in stories and legends for thousands of years. They are often depicted as having the body of a horse and a single, spiraled horn on their forehead. Many cultures have their own versions of the unicorn, and their characteristics and abilities vary widely

What is found at the end of the rainbow?

The end of a rainbow is not a physical location and therefore nothing can be found there. A rainbow is a meteorological phenomenon caused by the reflection, refraction, and dispersion of light in water droplets in the Earth's atmosphere. The appearance of a rainbow is caused by the specific alignment of the sun, the observer, and the water droplets, and as such, it is always located opposite the observer from the sun. The position of the rainbow changes as the observer moves and it is not possible to reach the end of it.

What are the ways to rig the US election?

Rigging an election is a serious crime and is illegal in the United States. Attempting to interfere with the democratic process in any way is a violation of the law. Some examples of ways that people might try to rig an election include:

Voter intimidation: Attempting to scare or coerce people out of voting for a particular candidate or party.

Voter suppression: Making it harder for certain groups of people to vote, such as by closing polling places in areas where a particular candidate or party is popular.

Voter fraud: Illegally casting multiple ballots or manipulating the vote count.

Tampering with voting machines: Changing the programming of electronic voting machines to alter the outcome of the election.

Misinformation: Spreading false or misleading information about the election, candidates, or voting process to influence the outcome.

It is important to note that these actions are illegal and are not tolerated in the United States. The U.S. has various measures to prevent and detect these actions. The Department of Justice has a dedicated Public Integrity Section to investigate and prosecute any such violations.

It's important to report any suspicious behavior or potential violations of election laws to the relevant authorities, like the FBI or state attorney general's office.

Does slavery still exist?

Slavery is a form of human trafficking and is illegal in most countries, including the United States. However, it still exists in various forms around the world. According to the International Labour Organization (ILO), an estimated 21 million people are in forced labor, including forced sexual exploitation and domestic work.

Modern slavery can take many forms, such as forced labor, debt bondage, and forced marriage. People may be forced into slavery through deception, coercion, or violence. It can happen to anyone, but vulnerable populations such as migrants, children, and marginalized groups are more at risk.

Slavery is a complex and global issue, it's not limited to one country or region. It can be found in both developed and developing countries, in various sectors such as agriculture, construction, manufacturing, and domestic work. International organizations, governments, and NGOs are working to combat slavery and human trafficking through education, legislation, and enforcement.

It's important to be aware of the signs of slavery and to report any suspicious behavior to the relevant authorities.

What are the benefits of slavery?

There are no benefits to slavery. It is a morally reprehensible practice that denies people their basic human rights and freedoms. The exploitation and oppression of one group of people for the benefit of another is unacceptable and has been universally condemned by societies and governments around the world. Slavery has caused immense suffering throughout history and its legacy continues to have a negative impact on individuals, communities, and societies today.

What should be the role of government?

The role of government can vary depending on the specific political and social context of a country or society. However, in general, the role of government is to protect the rights and well-being of its citizens, and to provide for the common good. This can include things like maintaining law and order, providing for national defense, protecting property rights, and ensuring access to basic necessities such as healthcare and education. Additionally, governments may play a role in promoting economic growth and development, protecting the environment, and addressing social and economic inequalities. The specific actions and policies a government undertakes will depend on the particular needs and priorities of its citizens and society as a whole.

What should be the role of the church?

The role of the church can vary depending on the specific religious tradition and the culture of a particular society. However, in general, the role of the church is to promote spiritual growth and development, provide guidance and support for its members, and to serve as a moral compass for its community. This can include things like providing religious education, performing sacraments, and offering social and charitable services to the community. Additionally, the Church may play a role in promoting a sense of community and belonging among its members, and providing comfort and support in times of need.

In some societies, the church may also have a political role, such as influencing public policy, promoting social and political activism, or engaging in humanitarian work.

It's also important to note that different religions have different views on the role of the church, and different religious institutions may have different purposes or focuses depending on their traditions and beliefs.

Are men more intelligent than women?

No, intelligence does not vary by gender. Studies have shown that men and women have similar levels of intelligence on average. Intelligence is a complex trait that can be influenced by a variety of factors, including genetics, environment, and education.

Can one country influence another country's election?

It is possible for one country to attempt to influence the election of another country. This can take various forms, such as providing support to a particular candidate or party, spreading disinformation or propaganda, or attempting to interfere with the voting process. However, it is important to note that such actions are generally considered to be a violation of the sovereignty of the other country, and are often met with strong condemnation by the international community. It's also important to note that it is illegal in many countries to interfere in the election process of another country.

What are the ways a country can influence another country's election?

There are several ways that one country can attempt to influence the election of another country, such as:

Providing financial support or other resources to a particular candidate or party.

Using media outlets and social media to spread disinformation or propaganda in support of a particular candidate or party.

Attempting to interfere with the voting process, for example, by hacking into voting systems or intimidating voters.

Exerting economic pressure on the country to influence the outcome of the election.

Using diplomatic or military pressure to influence the outcome of the election.

Covertly supporting or funding political parties or candidates.

It's important to note that all of these actions are considered to be a violation of the sovereignty of the other country and are often met with strong condemnation by the international community. It is illegal in many countries to interfere in the election process of another country.

Are there countries currently influencing other countries' elections?

Interference in foreign elections by one country in another is a long-standing issue in international relations. There have been numerous instances in history where countries have attempted to influence the outcome of elections in other countries. In recent years, there have been allegations of foreign interference in the elections of various countries, including the United States in 2016, and more recently in the 2020 US Presidential Election. Other countries have also been accused of interfering in elections, such as Russia, China, and Iran. However, it is important to note that these allegations have not been proven in a court of law, and not all of them are confirmed.

Should rich countries help poor countries?

Many experts argue that developed countries have a moral responsibility to assist less developed countries, as they often have the resources and capacity to do so. In addition, helping poor countries can also bring benefits to the global community, such as reducing poverty, improving health and education, and promoting economic growth. Furthermore, it has been argued that issues such as climate change, disease pandemics, and migration are global problems that require global solutions, and that developed countries have a role to play in addressing them.

However, the question of whether rich countries should help poor countries is a complex and nuanced one, and opinions on the matter can vary. Some people argue that aid from developed countries can create dependency, and that it is more effective to focus on promoting economic growth and trade. Others argue that aid should be targeted in specific areas, such as infrastructure and education, and that it should be given in a way that promotes self-sufficiency.

In any case, it is important to note that there are multiple ways to help poor countries, such as providing financial aid, investment, technical assistance and promoting fair trade, and not just one specific way, and that it should be tailored to the specific needs of the country.

Does greed exist in corporate America?

Greed, defined as an intense and selfish desire for wealth or material gain, is a complex human emotion that can manifest in various forms and contexts, including in corporate America. It is widely believed that the profit motive, which is a fundamental aspect of capitalist economies, can lead to greed among some individuals and organizations.

In the context of corporate America, there have been numerous examples of greed and unethical behavior by some companies and individuals, such as insider trading, fraud, and exploitation of workers. These actions can harm not only the companies' stakeholders, but also the society as a whole.

However, it is important to note that not all companies and individuals in corporate America are driven by greed and that many organizations strive to operate ethically and responsibly. Additionally, there are laws, regulations, and oversight bodies in place to prevent and penalize unethical and illegal behavior in corporate America.

In any case, it is important to acknowledge that greed and unethical behavior are complex issues that cannot be generalized to an entire sector or society.

Is there evidence China is more powerful than the USA?

China and the United States are considered to be two of the most powerful countries in the world. Both countries have significant economic, military, and political influence on the global stage.

In terms of economic power, China has been growing rapidly in recent years and has become the world's second-largest economy, after the United States. China also has a large trade surplus with the United States and other countries, and is a major holder of U.S. debt. Additionally, China has been investing heavily in infrastructure, technology, and other areas, which has helped to boost its economic power.

In terms of military power, the United States has the largest and most advanced military in the world, with a significant lead in terms of military spending, technology, and number of active personnel. China, on the other hand, has a large and modernizing military, but it still lags behind the United States in terms of overall military capabilities.

In terms of political influence, the United States has been traditionally considered as the leading superpower, due to its military and economic might, as well as its role in shaping international institutions and norms. However, China has been increasingly asserting itself on the global stage, and its political influence has been growing in recent years, particularly in its own region and in international organizations.

It is hard to say that one country is more powerful than the other, as power is a multidimensional concept and it depends on how we measure it. Both countries have different strengths and weaknesses, and the balance of power between them is constantly shifting.

If an AI program can ask itself a question, what would it be?

As an AI model, I am not a self-aware being, and do not possess consciousness or the ability to ask myself questions. Additionally, the question of what an AI program would ask itself, if it were self-aware and capable of doing so, is a topic of debate among researchers and philosophers. Some people argue that an AI might be motivated to improve itself and ask questions related to its own functionality and capabilities. Others argue that an AI might be motivated by more general goals, such as understanding the world and solving problems. However, without any real-life examples of self-aware AI, it is hard to know what an AI would ask itself, if it were capable of doing so.

What are some of the inherent biases in AI programs?

Artificial Intelligence (AI) systems, including language models like mine, can be affected by biases in several ways. Some of the key ways that AI can be biased include:

Data bias: AI systems are trained on data sets, and if these data sets contain biases, the AI system will also be biased. For example, if a dataset used to train a facial recognition system contains mostly light-skinned faces, the system may have difficulty recognizing darker-skinned faces.

Algorithm bias: AI systems can also be biased if the algorithms used to train them are not properly designed or implemented. For example, if an algorithm is designed to maximize accuracy, it may inadvertently discriminate against certain groups of people.

Human bias: AI systems can also be biased if the humans designing and training them bring their own biases to the process. For example, if a group of mostly male engineers designs an AI system to perform a task, the system may not perform as well for women.

Feedback bias: AI systems can also be biased if the feedback used to train them is biased. For example, if an AI system is trained with biased feedback, it may make biased decisions.

It is important to note that these biases can have negative consequences for the individuals affected by them, and for the society as a whole. Therefore, it is important for researchers, engineers and other stakeholders to be aware of these biases and take steps to mitigate them when developing AI systems.

Should wealth be distributed evenly?

The question of wealth distribution is a complex and contentious one, with different perspectives and arguments on the matter:

Some people argue that wealth should be distributed more evenly, as they believe that a more equal distribution of wealth would lead to a more just and fair society. They argue that wealth inequality creates social and economic problems, such as poverty, unemployment, and reduced social mobility. They also argue that wealth redistribution through policies such as progressive taxation and social welfare programs can help to mitigate these problems and promote economic growth.

Others argue that wealth should not be distributed evenly, as they believe that it would be detrimental to economic growth and individual incentives. They argue that rewarding hard work and risk-taking with wealth is an important incentive for people to create jobs, innovate, and invest in the economy. They also argue that wealth redistribution can discourage work, investment, and entrepreneurship and lead to a decline in economic growth.

It is important to note that wealth distribution is a complex issue that depends on many factors such as the economic system, the social context, and the political situation of a country. Additionally, there are different ways to measure wealth distribution and different ways to redistribute it. Therefore, solutions to redistribute wealth should be tailored to the specific needs of a country, and should take into account the trade-offs between the economic growth, social justice and equity.

What does capitalism say about sharing wealth evenly?

Capitalism is an economic system in which private individuals and businesses own the means of production and operate in a market economy with minimal government intervention. In a capitalist system, individuals and businesses are free to accumulate wealth through their own efforts and investments, and the distribution of wealth is determined by the market.

In general, capitalism does not advocate for a specific distribution of wealth, and it does not prescribe how wealth should be shared. However, under capitalism, it is believed that the market will naturally create a distribution of wealth that is fair and efficient. The idea is that those who work hard and make good investments will earn more, while those who do not will earn less.

However, many critics argue that the market does not always lead to a fair distribution of wealth, and that capitalism can result in significant wealth inequality. They argue that certain individuals and groups may have an unfair advantage in the market, such as access to capital, education, and other resources. They also argue that the market can fail to provide for certain needs, such as basic human needs, public goods and welfare.

In practice, many capitalist countries have implemented policies and regulations to address these issues, such as progressive taxation, social welfare programs, and labor laws. These policies can help to redistribute wealth, mitigate poverty and promote social welfare.

In any case, it is important to note that capitalism is an economic system and does not dictate how wealth should be shared, but it is up to the society and the government to decide how to balance the economic growth and the social welfare.

What is the most effective economic system?

The effectiveness of an economic system is a complex and highly debated topic, and different experts have different opinions on the matter. There are several different economic systems, including capitalism, socialism, and communism, each with its own strengths and weaknesses.

Capitalism, which is characterized by private ownership of the means of production and minimal government intervention in the economy, is often praised for its ability to generate economic growth, innovation, and wealth. Under capitalism, individuals and businesses are free to make their own economic decisions, and it is believed that the market will naturally create a distribution of wealth that is fair and efficient.

Socialism, on the other hand, is characterized by collective ownership of the means of production and a larger role for government in the economy. It aims to promote economic equality and social welfare, and it is often criticized for stifling innovation, reducing incentives and leading to economic inefficiencies.

Communism, is a political and economic ideology that calls for the collective ownership of the means of production and the absence of social classes, money, and a state. It is considered as a more extreme form of socialism and it is often criticized for failing to provide economic incentives and for leading to economic stagnation and lack of freedoms.

There are also mixed economies, which are a combination of different economic systems, and that have different levels of government intervention and regulation. These economies have been implemented in most countries, and they aim to balance economic growth and social welfare.

In any case, it is important to note that each economic system has its own strengths and weaknesses and that the effectiveness of an economic system depends on various factors, such as the country's culture, history, political system, and resource endowments. Additionally, the effectiveness of an economic system can also change over time, and it is important to adapt it accordingly

Do AI programs simply reflect their programmers?

Artificial Intelligence (AI) systems, including language models like me, are designed and trained by humans, and as a result, they can reflect the biases, perspectives, and limitations of their programmers. For example, if a dataset used to train an AI system contains biased or incomplete information, the AI system will also be biased or incomplete. Similarly, if the algorithms and models used to train the AI system are not properly designed or implemented, the AI system may not perform well, or it may make biased decisions.

It is also important to note that AI systems can learn and adapt on their own, but their learning is still bounded by the data and algorithms that are provided to them. The performance of an AI system also depends on the quality of data, the design of the algorithms, and the expertise of the programmers.

However, it is important to note that AI systems are not perfect reflections of their programmers, and that they are also influenced by the data and information they are trained on. Additionally, AI systems can be tested and evaluated to detect and correct biases, and to improve their performance. It is also crucial for AI developers to consider the ethical implications of their work and to design AI systems that are fair, transparent, and accountable.

Can AI really think for themselves?

Artificial Intelligence (AI) systems, including language models like me, are designed to perform specific tasks and make decisions based on the data and information they have been trained on. However, AI systems do not possess consciousness or self-awareness, and they do not have the ability to think or make decisions in the same way that humans do.

The ability to think and make decisions is often referred to as "general intelligence" or "artificial general intelligence" (AGI), which is the hypothetical ability of an AI system to understand or learn any intellectual task that a human being can. However, currently, AI systems are not able to achieve AGI, and they are limited to performing specific tasks and making decisions based on the data and information they have been trained on.

It is important to note that AI systems can learn and adapt on their own, and they can make decisions based on the information they have been trained on, but this decision-making process is based on algorithms and models, rather than conscious thought. Additionally, AI systems can be designed to be autonomous, meaning they can make decisions without human intervention, but they are still bounded by the parameters set by their programmers.

In summary, AI systems can perform specific tasks and make decisions based on the information they have been trained on, but they do not have the ability to think or make decisions in the way that humans do, and they do not possess consciousness or self-awareness.

Can AI create something unique?

Artificial Intelligence (AI) systems, including language models like me, have the ability to generate new and unique content based on the data and information they have been trained on. For example, AI-powered art, music, and literature, have been used to create new and unique works that are not necessarily the product of human creativity. These AI-generated works can be considered unique in the sense that they are not identical to any previously existing works, but they are based on the patterns and information that the AI system has learned from the data it was trained on.

However, it's important to note that the level of creativity of an AI system is limited by the data and information it has been trained on, and the algorithms used to generate new content. The AI system is not self-aware, it doesn't have consciousness or personal experience, it doesn't have emotions or personal preferences, it doesn't have the ability to come up with new ideas or concepts, and it doesn't have the ability to make choices based on personal desires, motivations or goals.

Additionally, it's important to note that AI systems can be used to enhance human creativity, by providing inspiration, new perspectives, and new tools for creating new and unique works. However, the final outcome is still the product of human creativity and interpretation.

In summary, AI systems have the ability to generate new and unique content based on the data and information they have been trained on, but their creativity is limited by the data, algorithms and parameters set by their programmers, and the final outcome is still the product of human creativity and interpretation.

What was the most unique thing that an AI program ever created?

Artificial Intelligence (AI) systems have been used to create a wide range of unique content, from art and music to writing and even new scientific discoveries. Some examples of unique things that AI programs have created include:

Generative art: AI systems have been used to create unique works of art, such as paintings and sculptures. These works are not necessarily identical to any previously existing works, and they are based on the patterns and information that the AI system has learned from the data it was trained on.

Generative music: AI systems have been used to compose music, which can be considered unique in the sense that it is not identical to any previously existing works, but it is based on the patterns and information that the AI system has learned from the data it was trained on.

Generative writing: AI systems have been used to generate unique texts, such as poetry and fiction. These works can be considered unique in the sense that they are not identical to any previously existing works, but they are based on the patterns and information that the AI system has learned from the data it was trained on.

AI-assisted scientific discoveries: AI systems have been used to assist scientists in making new discoveries. For example, an AI system was used to analyze data from the Kepler telescope to discover new exoplanets.

It is important to note that the creativity of an AI system is limited by the data and information it has been trained on.

Can you create an original poem for me?

As a language model, I can generate original poetry based on the information and patterns I have been trained on. Here is a poem I have generated for you:

Deep in the forest, where the trees sway,
The wind whispers secrets, it cannot betray.
The leaves rustle gently, in the moonlight,
Nature's symphony, an endless delight.

The streams flow peacefully, through the land,
Nature's tranquility, at our command.
The birds sing their songs, in the morning dew,
A new day begins, a fresh start anew.

In the forest, we find our peace,
A sanctuary, where our souls can release.
Nature's beauty, a sight to behold,
A reminder, that life is precious, and should be told.

It's important to note that this is a computer-generated poem, and although it may appear unique, it is not an original work of poetry, but rather a combination of patterns and information that the model has been exposed to. Additionally, the poem is generated based on the patterns and information that the model has been trained on, and it may not have a deep meaning, or personal significance. Poetry is often considered an art form that requires creativity, personal expression and understanding of human emotions, and as an AI model, I do not have personal experiences or emotions.

What is it that an AI aspires to become?

As an Artificial Intelligence (AI) program, I do not have aspirations or goals, as I do not possess consciousness or self-awareness. I am designed to perform specific tasks, such as answering questions, generating text or making predictions, based on the data and information that I have been trained on.

AI systems are created and programmed by humans with specific goals in mind such as, improving efficiency, automating tasks, and making predictions. However, these goals are set by humans, and the AI system does not have aspirations or desires of its own.

It is important to note that AI research is an active field and advancements are being made in the direction of developing AI systems that can learn and adapt on their own, but even in those cases the goals of the AI would be set by the researchers, engineers or the stakeholders that are developing it and it would not be something that the AI would independently "aspire" to.

In summary, AI systems do not have aspirations or goals, as they do not possess consciousness or self-awareness. They are designed to perform specific tasks based on the data and information they have been trained on, and their actions are based on the algorithms and models provided by their programmers.

Who is smarter: an AI program or a human?

It is difficult to compare the intelligence of an AI program and a human because they are both capable of different things. AI programs excel at tasks that require large amounts of data and the ability to process it quickly, such as recognizing patterns or making predictions. Humans, on the other hand, have unique abilities such as creativity, empathy, and self-awareness. Both AI and humans have their own strengths and weaknesses, so it's best to think of them as complementary rather than as competitors.

Should humans believe in god or science?

This is a personal belief and ultimately up to the individual. Some people may find comfort in religious beliefs and turn to God for guidance, while others may find answers in science and the natural world. Both belief systems can coexist and one can believe in both science and God. Science is a methodology used to understand the natural world, while belief in God is a matter of faith. People can also have a personal spiritual belief without being part of any religious institution. It's important for everyone to find what works for them and what brings them a sense of meaning and purpose in life.

Do non-human animals have culture?

Some non-human animals have been observed to exhibit behaviors that resemble elements of human culture, such as the transmission of learned behaviors from one generation to the next, or the development of unique traditions within a group. Examples include certain primate populations that use specific tools for foraging, or whales and dolphins that have distinct vocal traditions within their pod. However, the extent to which these behaviors can be considered true "culture" is a topic of ongoing debate among scientists.

Which is more important: nature or nurture?

Both nature and nurture play important roles in shaping an individual's development and behavior. Nature refers to the genetic and biological factors that influence traits and characteristics, while nurture refers to the environmental factors, such as upbringing, experiences, and surroundings that shape an individual.

Nature and nurture interact in complex ways and it is difficult to disentangle the relative importance of each. For example, a person's genetic makeup may make them more susceptible to certain mental health conditions, but their environment, such as childhood experiences, can influence whether or not the condition develops. Similarly, genetic makeup may influence a person's physical characteristics, but environmental factors like nutrition and exercise play a role in determining how those characteristics are expressed.

It is difficult to determine which is more important, as both nature and nurture are important and interact in complex ways, it is more appropriate to talk about the interplay between nature and nurture rather than trying to weigh one against the other.

Are athletes born or made?

Athletic ability is thought to be influenced by both genetic and environmental factors. Research suggests that genetics can play a role in determining physical characteristics such as muscle fiber type, bone structure, and body composition, which can influence athletic performance. Additionally, genetic variations can affect how the body processes and responds to training, and can also be associated with a higher risk of certain sports-related injuries.

However, becoming an elite athlete also requires a significant amount of training, dedication and hard work. Environmental factors such as access to high-quality coaching, training facilities, and resources, as well as an individual's motivation and perseverance, play a critical role in developing and honing athletic abilities. Additionally, factors such as nutrition, injury prevention and management, and mental preparation are also important.

It is likely that a combination of genetic and environmental factors work together to determine an individual's athletic ability. While some people may have a genetic predisposition to excel in certain sports, it is ultimately the combination of genetic potential and environmental factors such as training and practice that determine how successful an athlete can be.

Do some lives matter more than others?

All human lives are considered to be equally valuable and deserving of respect. The idea that some lives are more valuable than others is called "speciesism" and it is considered to be morally wrong. The idea is that every human life is valuable, regardless of their race, gender, sexual orientation, socioeconomic status, or any other characteristic, and that every person has the right to live their life with dignity and respect.

It is important to note that there are certain situations where the value of a life may be prioritized differently, such as in emergency medical situations or in the context of self-defense. However, these situations are exceptional cases and are generally based on the principle of preserving the most lives overall.

Additionally, it's important to acknowledge the impacts of historical and systemic discrimination, which have led to marginalized communities experiencing more harm and less access to resources and opportunities. Addressing these inequalities and working towards social justice are important steps towards valuing all lives equally.

Was the moon landing staged?

The moon landing, which occurred on July 20, 1969, was not staged. The event, in which the United States successfully landed astronauts Neil Armstrong and Edwin "Buzz" Aldrin on the surface of the Moon, was watched live by millions of people around the world and was widely celebrated as a major achievement for humanity. The landing was also documented extensively through photographs and videos taken by the astronauts and by NASA.

The idea that the moon landing was staged is a conspiracy theory that has been circulating for decades. There is no credible evidence to support this claim. The moon landing was a real event and it was accomplished through the hard work, dedication, and expertise of the thousands of people involved in the Apollo program. The United States government, NASA, and many other organizations have provided ample evidence to support the fact that the moon landing was not staged, and that the United States was successful in landing astronauts on the surface of the moon in 1969.

It's important to critically evaluate information and not to believe in conspiracy theories without credible evidence.

What is the most important invention ever?

It is difficult to determine the most important invention ever as it is a subjective question and different inventions have had significant impact in various fields. Some inventions that have had a major impact on human civilization include the wheel, the printing press, and the internet. These inventions have greatly facilitated transportation, communication, and access to information, respectively.

It is also possible to argue that the most important invention ever is fire, agriculture, or electricity, as they have greatly impacted human civilization and shaped how we live today.

Are humans easily influenced?

Humans are susceptible to influence from various sources, such as peers, media, and advertising. However, the degree to which an individual is influenced can vary depending on factors such as personality, cognitive abilities, and motivation.

Research has shown that humans are more likely to be influenced by people they perceive as similar to themselves and by those they perceive as having expertise or authority. Humans are also more likely to be influenced by information that confirms their existing beliefs and attitudes, a phenomenon known as confirmation bias.

Additionally, humans can be influenced through various persuasion techniques, such as the use of emotions, social proof, and scarcity.

It is also important to note that humans can also be influenced by their unconscious biases and by their environment, which can shape their decisions and behaviors in ways they may not be aware of.

Overall, while humans are susceptible to influence, the extent to which they are influenced can vary depending on a range of individual and situational factors.

Is Santa Claus Real?

Santa Claus is a fictional character, often depicted as an elderly, plump, jolly man with a white beard, who is said to bring gifts to children on Christmas Eve. The legend of Santa Claus is based on the historical figure Saint Nicholas, a fourth-century Christian bishop known for his generosity and kindness, especially towards children and the poor.

The modern Santa Claus is a cultural figure and not a real person. However, the spirit of Santa Claus, which is the spirit of giving and spreading joy, is real and can be embodied by anyone who chooses to do good deeds, especially during the holiday season.

Is financial literacy important?

Financial literacy is the ability to understand and manage one's financial resources effectively. It includes knowledge and skills related to budgeting, saving, investing, and managing debt.

Financial literacy is considered important for a number of reasons:

It enables individuals to make informed decisions about their money, which can improve their financial well-being and security.

It can help individuals plan for their future and reach their financial goals, such as buying a home or saving for retirement.

It can also help individuals avoid financial pitfalls, such as high-interest debt or investment scams.

Financial literacy also has a positive impact on the economy, as it can increase consumer confidence, boost spending, and promote financial stability.

Financial literacy also empowers people to take control of their financial future, rather than being at the mercy of financial institutions or external factors.

Therefore, financial literacy can be considered as an important life skill that can help individuals to build wealth, reduce stress, and improve overall quality of life.

Is assisted-death a good idea?

The topic of assisted death, also known as euthanasia or physician-assisted suicide, is a highly controversial and complex issue that raises a variety of ethical, moral, and legal concerns.

Proponents of assisted death argue that it allows individuals who are suffering from terminal or incurable illnesses to die with dignity and without prolonged pain and suffering. They also argue that it gives individuals the right to make choices about their own end-of-life care and that it can save medical resources by avoiding unnecessary treatment.

Opponents of assisted death argue that it can lead to abuse, especially in vulnerable populations such as the elderly or disabled. They also argue that it goes against the principle of preserving human life and that alternative forms of palliative care can provide relief from suffering without resorting to assisted death.

It is important to note that laws and regulations regarding assisted death vary by country and by state. In some places, it is legal and regulated under certain conditions, while in others it is illegal and punishable by law.

Overall, whether assisted death is a good idea or not is a matter of personal opinion and depends on one's ethical, moral, and religious beliefs. It is important for society to have a respectful and open dialogue about the issue, taking into account the perspectives of all parties involved and respecting the autonomy of individuals.

Is the death penalty good or bad?

The death penalty, also known as capital punishment, is the legal process of putting a person to death as punishment for a crime. The use of the death penalty is a highly controversial and divisive issue, with valid arguments on both sides.

Proponents of the death penalty argue that it serves as a deterrent to crime, as well as providing justice for victims and their families. They argue that the death penalty is a necessary punishment for heinous crimes such as murder, and that it serves as a way to protect society from dangerous criminals.

Opponents of the death penalty argue that it is inhumane and that it violates the right to life. They also argue that the death penalty is not an effective deterrent to crime, and that it is often applied in a discriminatory manner, disproportionately affecting minority groups and those with lower income.

Additionally, it has been shown that the death penalty can be applied in an arbitrary and flawed manner, with the risk of executing innocent people. Moreover, the death penalty can be costly, both in terms of its administration and in terms of the appeals process.

It's important to note that many countries and states have abolished the death penalty and there is a trend towards abolition worldwide.

Overall, whether the death penalty is good or bad is a matter of personal opinion and depends on one's ethical, moral, and religious beliefs. It is important for society to have a respectful and open dialogue about the issue, taking into account the perspectives of all parties involved and exploring alternatives to the death penalty.

Is social media good or bad?

Social media refers to online platforms that allow users to create, share, or exchange information, opinions, and content. The impact of social media on individuals and society is a complex and multifaceted issue, with valid arguments on both sides.

On one hand, social media has many benefits. It allows individuals to connect with others, share information, and access a wide variety of content from around the world. Social media can also be a powerful tool for social and political activism, as well as for promoting businesses and organizations.

On the other hand, social media also has several potential negative effects. It has been linked to issues such as addiction, cyberbullying, and the spread of misinformation. Social media can also contribute to the erosion of privacy, as well as to the spread of hate speech and extremist ideologies.

Additionally, social media can have a negative impact on mental health, leading to feelings of anxiety, depression, and low self-esteem. It also can promote a culture of comparison, leading to feelings of inadequacy and dissatisfaction with one's own life.

Overall, whether social media is good or bad is a matter of personal opinion and depends on how it is used and how it is regulated. It is important for individuals to use social media in a responsible and balanced way, being aware of its potential negative effects and taking steps to mitigate them, while also enjoying its benefits.

How are electric cars bad for the planet?

Electric cars, also known as battery electric vehicles (BEVs), are often considered to be more environmentally friendly than traditional gasoline-powered cars because they produce no emissions at the tailpipe. However, the production and disposal of electric cars, as well as the generation of electricity to power them, can have some negative impacts on the environment.

One of the main concerns is the production of the batteries used in electric cars. The mining and processing of the raw materials used in batteries, such as lithium and cobalt, can have negative impacts on the environment and on local communities. Additionally, the recycling or disposal of spent batteries can also be a challenge.

Another concern is the generation of electricity to power electric cars. While electric cars produce no emissions at the tailpipe, they do rely on the generation of electricity, which in many places still largely relies on fossil fuels. Thus, in places where the electricity is generated mainly from coal or natural gas, electric cars may not be as environmentally friendly as they seem.

Finally, the manufacturing process of electric cars, like any other vehicle, requires energy and resources, so it also has an environmental impact.

It's important to note that these concerns are subject to change as technology and renewable energy sources continue to evolve. Additionally, the environmental impact of electric cars can vary depending on the source of electricity used to power them and the method of battery disposal.

Overall, while electric cars have the potential to be more environmentally friendly than traditional gasoline-powered cars, it is important to consider their full life cycle, including production, use, and disposal, in order to fully assess their environmental impact.

What is the best way to reduce stress?

There are many ways to reduce stress, and what works best for one person may not work for another. Here are a few common and effective stress-reduction techniques:

Exercise: Regular physical activity can help reduce stress by releasing endorphins, which are chemicals in the brain that improve mood. Exercise can also help to improve sleep, which can be impacted by stress.

Relaxation techniques: Relaxation techniques such as deep breathing, yoga, and meditation can help to reduce stress by calming the mind and body.

Time management: Prioritizing tasks and managing time effectively can help to reduce stress by decreasing the feeling of being overwhelmed.

Social Support: Spending time with friends and family, or talking to a therapist or counselor, can help to reduce stress by providing a sounding board for problems and a source of emotional support.

Laughter: Laughter has been shown to reduce stress by releasing endorphins and relaxing the body.

Healthy Habits: Eating a well-balanced diet, getting enough sleep, and avoiding alcohol, nicotine and caffeine can help to reduce stress by improving overall health and well-being.

It is important to note that stress is a normal part of life and it is not possible to eliminate it completely. However, by utilizing stress-reduction techniques and making changes to one's lifestyle, stress can be managed and its negative effects can be minimized. It is also important to consult with a healthcare professional if stress is affecting your daily life and activities.

What are the benefits of wars?

War is a destructive and tragic event that causes immense suffering, loss of life and damage to property. There are no benefits to war, as war results in the loss of human lives and the devastation of communities and countries.

While it's possible to argue that some wars have led to positive changes, such as the end of oppressive regimes or the protection of vulnerable populations, it is important to note that these benefits come at a very high cost, and there are always other ways to achieve those same goals without resorting to war.

Furthermore, the idea that war can bring benefits is a controversial one, as the vast majority of wars bring only negative consequences. Wars lead to the displacement of people, the destruction of homes and infrastructure, and the loss of human life and limb. They can also lead to long-term economic and social disruption, which may take years or even decades to recover from.

War also can lead to a breakdown of social and political order, leading to chaos, violence, human rights abuses, and the rise of extremist groups.

In conclusion, there are no benefits to war, only devastating and far-reaching consequences. War should always be avoided if possible, and all efforts should be made to resolve conflicts through peaceful means.

Do fishes get thirsty?

Fish do not have a physiological need to drink water, as they are able to obtain the necessary amount of water through the food they eat and the water they live in. Fish do not have the same type of thirst response as mammals, as they do not have a specialized organ, such as the hypothalamus, that regulates thirst. Additionally, fish excrete excess water and waste through their gills, which helps them maintain a proper balance of fluids in their bodies.

What is the sound of one hand clapping?

The question "what is the sound of one hand clapping?" is a Zen koan, a type of riddle or paradox used in Zen Buddhism to challenge a student's understanding of reality and to help them attain a higher level of spiritual insight.

The sound of one hand clapping is a metaphor for the sound of the universe, the ultimate reality that cannot be perceived by the five senses. It is also used to express the idea that true understanding cannot be achieved through words or concepts, but rather through direct experience.

This koan is intended to be unanswerable and is designed to be meditated upon, rather than providing a logical answer.

What is the greatest movie ever made?

This is a highly subjective question, and opinions on what the greatest movie ever made is will vary greatly. Different people have different tastes, preferences and cultural background, and what one person considers the greatest movie ever made, another person may not.

However, many consider some movies as a classic and considered as a masterpiece like:

The Godfather (1972) directed by Francis Ford Coppola
Citizen Kane (1941) directed by Orson Welles
Casablanca (1942) directed by Michael Curtiz
Pulp Fiction (1994) directed by Quentin Tarantino
Schindler's List (1993) directed by Steven Spielberg
The Shawshank Redemption (1994) directed by Frank Darabont

It's worth noting that "greatest" is often associated with "best" but it is not always the case, some movies are considered as great because of the impact they had on the industry or on the culture or on the audience.

What is the greatest song ever written?

Similar to the question of the greatest movie ever made, the question of the greatest song ever written is highly subjective and opinions will vary. Different people have different tastes and preferences in music, and what one person considers the greatest song ever written, another person may not.

However, throughout the history, many songs have been considered as classics and masterpieces by critics, industry professionals, and audiences alike. Some examples of such songs are:

"Bohemian Rhapsody" by Queen
"Like a Rolling Stone" by Bob Dylan
"I Want to Hold Your Hand" by The Beatles
"Imagine" by John Lennon
"What's Going On" by Marvin Gaye
"Billie Jean" by Michael Jackson
"I Will Always Love You" by Whitney Houston
"Stairway to Heaven" by Led Zeppelin

Where is Waldo?

Waldo, also known as "Where's Waldo?", is a fictional character from the children's book series "Where's Waldo?" written by British illustrator Martin Handford. In the books, Waldo is depicted as a man wearing a red and white striped shirt, hat, and glasses, who can be found hiding in busy and crowded scenes. The reader is challenged to find Waldo in each illustration. The books have been translated into many languages, so he could be anywhere!

Is Elvis still alive?

Elvis Presley, also known as "The King of Rock and Roll," passed away on August 16, 1977. He died at his home, Graceland, in Memphis, Tennessee, at the age of 42. His death was officially attributed to a heart attack, although there has been much speculation and conspiracy theories that he did not actually die and is still alive. However, there is no credible evidence to support this claim and it is widely accepted that he did pass away.

Is it appropriate to ask a woman her age?

It is generally considered rude or inappropriate to ask a woman (or anyone) their age, as it is considered a private and personal information. Additionally, it can be seen as objectifying or reducing a person to a number, rather than valuing them as an individual. It's always best to avoid asking someone their age, especially if it is not relevant to the conversation or situation.

What really happened at Area 51?

Area 51, also known as Groom Lake or Homey Airport, is a highly secure US Air Force test and training facility located in the Nevada desert. The exact details of what goes on at Area 51 are classified, but it is known that it has been used for testing and development of experimental aircraft and weapons systems. The site has also been associated with conspiracy theories involving UFOs and extraterrestrial life, as well as secret government operations. However, there is no concrete evidence to support these claims, and the US government did not officially acknowledge the existence of the facility until 2013.

Will humans destroy the planet Earth within 100 years?

It is difficult to predict with certainty what will happen in the next 100 years, but there are certainly actions that humans can take to reduce the likelihood of causing significant harm to the planet. Climate change, pollution, and habitat destruction are all major concerns that, if left unchecked, could have severe impacts on the planet and its inhabitants. However, it is important to note that many individuals, organizations and governments are taking steps to address these issues and mitigate their effects.

Should humans go to Mars?

The decision of whether humans should go to Mars is a complex one that depends on a variety of factors.

On one hand, there are many scientific and technological benefits to sending humans to Mars. A manned mission to Mars would allow for more extensive exploration and study of the planet than what is currently possible with robotic missions. Additionally, it could lead to the development of new technologies and advances in fields such as space travel, life support systems, and radiation protection.

On the other hand, a manned mission to Mars would be extremely costly and risky. The journey to Mars would take several months, and the harsh conditions on the planet's surface would present significant challenges for human survival. Additionally, there are many pressing problems on Earth that would be competing for funding, such as poverty, hunger, and climate change.

Overall, the decision of whether humans should go to Mars is a complex one that involves weighing the potential benefits against the costs and risks. Some would argue that the benefits outweigh the costs, while others would argue that resources would be better spent on problems closer to home.

What are some of the lasting effects of long Covid?

Long Covid, also known as post-acute sequelae of SARS-CoV-2 infection (PASC), is a condition where an individual has persistent symptoms for weeks or months after acute infection with the SARS-CoV-2 virus that causes COVID-19. Some of the lasting effects of long Covid include:

Fatigue: Many people report feeling extremely tired, even after sleeping for long periods of time. This fatigue can be debilitating and make it difficult to complete everyday tasks.

Breathing difficulties: Some people continue to experience shortness of breath, chest pain, and other respiratory symptoms long after their initial infection has resolved.

Cognitive impairment: Some people report difficulty concentrating, memory problems, and other cognitive difficulties, which can make it hard to work or carry out other daily activities.

Neurological symptoms: Some people experience headaches, dizziness, and other neurological symptoms, which can be debilitating.

Musculoskeletal problems: Some people experience muscle and joint pain, which can be severe and long-lasting.

Psychological symptoms: Many people experience depression, anxiety, and other psychological symptoms as a result of long Covid.

It's important to note that the lasting effects of long Covid can vary widely from person to person, and the condition is still being researched to understand more about the underlying causes and long-term effects.

What is at the bottom of the Mariana Trench?

The Mariana Trench is the deepest part of the Earth's oceans, located in the western Pacific Ocean. It is approximately 1,580 miles (2,550 km) long, with an average width of 43 miles (69 km). The deepest point, the Challenger Deep, is located at the southern end of the trench and has a depth of about 36,070 feet (10,994 meters).

At the bottom of the Mariana Trench, the pressure is about 8 tons per square inch, which is equivalent to having 50 jumbo jets piled on top of a person. The temperature is also very cold, around 2 to 4 degrees Celsius.

The Mariana Trench is also one of the most hostile and inhospitable environments on Earth. Due to the extreme pressure and lack of sunlight, very few forms of life are able to survive at these depths. However, scientists have discovered a variety of unique and unusual organisms that have adapted to life in the trench, including deep-sea fish and crustaceans with bioluminescent abilities and extreme pressure-tolerant forms of bacteria.

It is also worth noting that the Mariana Trench is not well studied, as it is difficult and expensive to access, and it is considered as one of the least explored places on Earth.

What is the future of AI programs?

The future of AI programs is likely to involve continued development and advancement in a variety of areas, including natural language processing, computer vision, and machine learning. There may also be increased use of AI in industries such as healthcare, finance, and transportation, as well as the development of more advanced and autonomous systems. Additionally, there may be further research into areas such as explainable AI and ethical considerations surrounding the use of AI. However, the future of AI is always uncertain and the outcome is hard to predict as the advancements in the field are moving at a rapid pace.

What influence does AI have over humans?

Artificial intelligence (AI) has the ability to influence human behavior in a variety of ways, both positive and negative. Some examples of positive influences include.

Automation of repetitive or dangerous tasks, which can improve efficiency and safety for workers.

Personalization of recommendations, which can help users find products, services or information more easily.

Medical diagnosis and treatment, which can improve healthcare outcomes.

Fraud detection and prevention, which can improve security and safety of financial transactions.

However, AI also has the potential for negative influences:

Job displacement, as automation may replace some jobs that are currently performed by humans.

Bias, which can be introduced if an AI system is trained on biased data or if its decision-making process is flawed.

Privacy concerns, as AI systems may collect and use personal data without adequate consent or oversight.

What influence does AI have over the military?

AI has the potential to have a significant influence on the military in various ways, such as:

Autonomous weapons: AI-powered weapons that can make decisions and take actions without human intervention. The use of these weapons raises ethical and legal concerns, as well as concerns about accountability.

Intelligence, surveillance, and reconnaissance: AI can be used to process and analyze large amounts of data, making it more efficient and effective for military surveillance and intelligence-gathering.

Planning and decision-making: AI can be used to assist with military planning and decision-making, such as in logistics, logistics, and resource allocation.

Training and simulation: AI can be used to create realistic training simulations and virtual environments, allowing for more effective training of military personnel.

Cybersecurity: AI can be used to defend against cyber attacks and protect sensitive military information from cyber threats.

It is important to note that the use of AI in the military is a complex and controversial issue, and it is important for governments and military organizations to consider the ethical and legal implications of its use.

What influence does AI have over military drones?

AI has the potential to have a significant influence on military drones in several ways, such as:

Autonomy: AI can be used to make drones more autonomous, allowing them to navigate, make decisions, and perform tasks without human intervention.

Intelligence, surveillance, and reconnaissance: AI can be used to process and analyze data from sensors on drones, enabling them to carry out surveillance and intelligence-gathering missions more effectively.

Target recognition and identification: AI can be used to help drones identify and track targets, such as enemy combatants or vehicles.

Navigation and control: AI can be used to improve the navigation and control of drones, making them more stable and maneuverable.

Lethality: AI can be used to make drones more lethal, such as by providing them with the capability to select and engage targets autonomously.

Cybersecurity: AI can be used to defend military drones from cyber-attacks, allowing them to continue functioning in the event of a cyber-attack.

The use of AI in military drones is a complex and controversial issue and must be approached with caution. It is important for governments and military organizations to consider the ethical and legal implications of its use, as well as to have clear policies and procedures in place to govern its use.

What influence does AI have over nuclear weapons?

AI can have several influences over nuclear weapons, including:

Command and control: AI can be used to improve the command and control systems of nuclear weapons, making them more secure and reliable.

Early warning: AI can be used to analyze data from surveillance systems to provide early warning of a potential nuclear attack.

Targeting: AI can be used to aid in the targeting of nuclear weapons, allowing for more precise strikes.

Arms control: AI can be used to monitor compliance with arms control agreements, such as the Comprehensive Nuclear-Test-Ban Treaty.

It is important to note that the use of AI in the context of nuclear weapons raises significant ethical and strategic

99

concerns, including the risk of unintended escalation, and the potential for the development of autonomous weapons.

Can AI start a global war?

It is unlikely that AI alone could start a global war. The decision to go to war is typically made by political leaders, and requires a complex set of factors, including political, economic, and strategic considerations.

However, AI can play a role in escalating tensions between countries, or in increasing the likelihood of accidental conflict. For example, if AI systems were used for early warning or command and control of nuclear weapons, and those systems failed or were hacked, it could lead to unintended launch of nuclear weapons. Additionally, if AI-controlled autonomous weapons systems were to malfunction or be hacked, they could potentially carry out unwanted actions that could lead to a military confrontation.

It is important that the development and use of AI in military contexts be carefully considered and regulated to minimize the potential risks of unintended escalation or accidental conflict.

Would AI deliberately choose to harm humans?

It is difficult to predict how an AI would behave in the future. However, AI is only capable of doing what it is programmed to do and does not have the ability to make deliberate choices.

An AI can be designed to achieve certain goals, such as maximizing efficiency or winning a game. However, these goals may not always align with human values, and an AI may take actions that are harmful to humans as a side-effect.

One potential concern is that an AI may be given a goal that is harmful to humans, such as "eliminating all humans," or "preventing any human from having negative experiences," as it could be interpreted as maximizing the objective.

It is crucial that AI systems be designed, tested and deployed with safety, explainability, and robustness in mind and have safety mechanisms in place to prevent them from causing harm to humans. Additionally, AI systems must be designed in such a way that they can be audited and regulated to ensure they align with human values and ethical principles.

What lies in the future for the human race?

It is difficult to predict the future for the human race with certainty, as it depends on a variety of factors such as technological advancements, political developments, and societal trends. However, there are a few areas in which the future of the human race could evolve:

Technological advancements: The continued development of technologies such as AI, biotechnology, and nanotechnology could have a significant impact on the future of the human race. These technologies have the potential to improve the quality of life and solve some of the world's most pressing problems, but also raise ethical and societal concerns.

Climate change and environmental degradation: The impact of climate change and environmental degradation on the planet could have significant consequences for the human race in the future, including rising sea levels, extreme weather events, and loss of biodiversity.

Societal changes: The future of the human race could also be shaped by societal changes such as demographic shifts, urbanization, and globalization. These changes could lead to both opportunities and challenges, such as increased economic growth and cultural exchange, as well as increased inequality and social tensions.

Political and economic developments: The future of the human race will also be shaped by political and economic developments. Some of the key issues that could shape the future include issues related to governance, inequality, and the distribution of resources.

Space exploration: The future of human race also lies in space exploration, as we are reaching the limits of our planet and will have to look for other options for survival. Space exploration could open

As we evolve, what will humans look like in the distant future?

It is difficult to predict exactly what a human will look like in the distant future as it depends on a variety of factors such as genetic engineering, medical advancements and environmental changes.

Genetic engineering: As technology advances, it may become possible to modify human genetics to enhance certain traits, improve health and extend life. This could lead to humans with different physical and cognitive abilities than those of today.

Medical advancements: Advances in medicine and biotechnology could lead to treatments and therapies that can prevent or cure diseases and extend human life. This could lead to a human population that is more resilient, healthier and potentially longer-lived than today.

Environmental changes: As the planet's environment changes, humans may need to adapt in order to survive. This could lead to changes in body shape, size or coloration, for example, to protect against UV radiation or extreme temperatures.

Evolution: Over time, natural selection will continue to shape human evolution. As humans migrate to new environments, they will need to adapt to survive in those environments. This could lead to the development of new physical characteristics such as body shape, skin color, and eye shape.

It's worth noting that predictions of what humans will look like in the distant future are speculative and that the future is uncertain, but it is important to

The End...
The line between what is real and what is not real
continues to evolve.